Jane Goodall

Terry Barber

ACTIVIST
SERIES

Jane Goodall is published by
Grass Roots Press, a division of Literacy Services of Canada Ltd.

PHONE 1–888–303–3213
WEBSITE www.literacyservices.com

ACKNOWLEDGEMENTS

We would like to thank The Jane Goodall Institute of Canada for supplying the majority of the photographs. For more information, visit the Jane Goodall website at: www.janegoodall.ca

We acknowledge the financial support of the Government of Canada through the Book Publishing Industry Development Program (BPIDP) for our publishing activities.

We acknowledge the support of the Alberta Foundation for the Arts for our publishing programs.

Editor: Dr. Pat Campbell
Image Research: Dr. Pat Campbell
Book design: Lara Minja, Lime Design Inc.

Library and Archives Canada Cataloguing in Publication

Barber, Terry, date
    Jane Goodall / Terry Barber.

(Activist series)
ISBN 1–894593–43–X

    1. Goodall, Jane, 1934–. 2. Primatologists—England—Biography.
3. Readers for new literates. I. Title. II. Series.

QL31.G58B37 2006   428.6'2   C2005–907553–8

Printed in Canada

Contents

Jane holds out her hand to a chimpanzee.

Jane's Special Moment

The year is 1961. Jane Goodall sits and watches the **chimpanzee.** The male chimp sits beside her. Jane calls him David Greybeard. Jane puts a nut in her hand. She holds out her hand to David.

Chimpanzees are also called chimps.

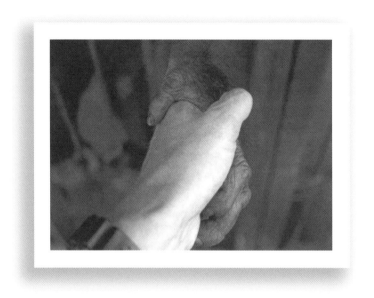

Jane and David Greybeard hold hands.

Jane's Special Moment

David does not want the nut.
David takes Jane's hand in his hand.
She feels his gentle touch. She feels his
soft fingers. This is special for Jane.
A chimpanzee accepts her.

David Greybeard was the first chimpanzee to trust Jane.

Jane sits with David Greybeard.

Jane's Special Moment

Months spent walking in thick forests seem worth it. Months spent working in rain and heat seem worth it. Jane is thinking: "This is where I belong. This is what I came into the world to do."

Jane watches chimpanzees.

Even as a child, Jane loved animals.

Jane as a Child

Jane is born in England in 1934. She grows up before there are TVs and computers. Jane loves animals. She likes playing outdoors. Jane likes reading outdoors. Jane's family does not have a lot of money. Jane does not care. Jane has happy times as a child.

Jane hugs Jubilee, her toy chimp.

Jane's dream comes true. Jane climbs a tree in Africa. Jane is looking for chimpanzees.

Jane as a Child

Jane climbs her favourite tree. She sits on a branch. The wind touches her. The sun warms her. Birds sing. Jane dreams of going to Africa. She wants to live with the animals.

Jane likes to read Tarzan books.

Jane Goodall and Dr. Louis Leakey

Jane Goes to Africa

Jane works and saves her money. Jane goes to Africa at the age of 23. She meets Dr. Louis Leakey. He is famous. He is a scientist. Louis studies early humans. Louis sees something special in Jane. He wants her to become a scientist. Louis wants Jane to study chimpanzees.

Africa

Jane studies chimps in Gombe.

Jane Goes to Africa

Jane agrees to study chimpanzees.
She knows it will be a hard job.
The chimpanzees do not live in zoos.
They live in the wild. They live in
thick forests. They are hard to study.
Jane needs to work hard to learn
about the chimpanzees.

This chimpanzee lives in the wild.

Jane is looking for chimpanzees high in the trees.

Jane watches the chimpanzees.

Jane Returns to School

Jane studies chimpanzees in the wild. This is called **fieldwork**. It costs a lot of money to do fieldwork. Jane needs more education to get **grants**.

Jane decides to become a scientist. She goes to university when she is 28. She works hard and gets her **Ph.D**. People call her Dr. Jane Goodall.

A group of chimps walk in the forest.

The Chimpanzees

Dr. Jane Goodall has studied chimpanzees since 1960. She learns many things. Jane learns that chimps live in groups. Each group has a leader. Each chimp has a place in the group.

A mother chimp and her baby.

The Chimpanzees

Jane learns that baby chimps need their mothers. Just as human babies do. Young chimps drink their mother's milk for at least three years. Baby chimps stay with their mothers for seven to eight years.

This chimp builds a nest.

A chimp sits in her bed at night.

The Chimpanzees

Jane watches the chimps at night.
They make beds in trees. They make
beds out of twigs and branches.
The chimps are safer in the trees.

Jane names this chimp Patti.

Jane names this chimp Sherry.

Jane names this chimp Mike.

Jane's Work

Jane is the first scientist to give names to animals. She gives names to the animals she studies. Before Jane's work, other scientists did not use names. They used numbers. This shows that Jane is a free thinker. She does things her way.

This chimpanzee is mad.

Jane's Work

Jane learns that chimpanzees are not all the same. David Greybeard is different from other chimps. He is very calm. Some chimps are not calm. Some chimps are brave. Some are shy. Some are patient. Some have tempers.

A sad chimpanzee sits on the ground.

Jane's Work

We now know that animals have feelings. Jane's work with chimpanzees shows us that chimps have feelings. When a chimp dies, the other chimpanzees are sad. Just as humans are sad when someone dies.

A sad chimpanzee lies in the grass.

This chimp's name is Baluku. He is eating berries.

Jane's Work

Jane watches the chimps eat. Chimps spend up to seven hours a day eating. They eat many different foods. They climb trees to find figs. Honey tastes good to chimps. So do leaves and flowers.

This chimp's name is Figan. He is eating figs.

This chimp's name
is Fifi. She is eating
meat.

This chimp
is eating a
bushbuck.

Jane's Work

Jane watches chimps hunt, kill, and eat small animals. Jane is the first scientist to see a chimp hunt and eat meat.

This chimp is eating a monkey.

This chimp's name is Eddie.
He uses a stick as a tool.

Jane's Work

Jane discovers that chimps make and use tools. They use tools to eat and drink. They use tools to scare other animals.

Chimps make tools out of sticks, twigs, leaves, and rocks.

A chimp uses a twig to look for ants.

Jane's Work

A chimpanzee uses a twig to catch ants. The chimp pushes the twig into the ant hole. The ants climb the twig. Then, the chimp eats the ants. Chimps use leaves to soak up water. Then they suck the water out of the leaves.

A chimp is sucking water out of leaves.

Chimpanzees have strong family ties.

Humans and Chimpanzees

Jane has taught us that chimpanzees are like humans. They have families. They love their children. They can think. They have feelings. They feel pain.

This chimpanzee lives in a small cage.
This is an awful life for any animal.

Humans and Chimpanzees

Animals can feel pain. Humans cause much of this pain. We put animals in zoos. We put animals in the circus. We study animals in labs. We often work animals too hard. Animals are badly treated by humans. Humans need to stop hurting animals.

A chimpanzee as it should be: free and wild.

Animals Have Rights

Chimpanzees and all other animals have rights. A right to live. A right to live free. People need to protect animals. We must respect animals' needs and feelings. Wild animals make our world a better place to live in.

Glossary

bushbuck: a small antelope that lives in parts of Africa.

chimpanzee: an ape that lives in parts of Africa.

fieldwork: scientists watch chimps and take notes in the wild. This is an example of fieldwork.

grant: a gift of money.

Ph.D.: these three letters mean Doctor of Philosophy.

Talking About the Book

What did you learn about Jane Goodall?

What did you learn about chimpanzees?

Why did the author call Jane a
"free thinker"?

How do you think Jane has made
the world a better place?

Picture Credits